Let's Look at Light

Where Does Light Come From?

by Mari Schuh

PEBBLE
a capstone imprint

Pebble Plus is published by Pebble
1710 Roe Crest Drive, North Mankato, Minnesota 56003
www.mycapstone.com

Library of Congress Cataloging-in-Publication Data
Names: Schuh, Mari C., 1975- author.
Title: Where does light come from? / by Mari Schuh.
Description: North Mankato, Minnesota : Pebble, a Capstone imprint, [2020] | Series: Pebble plus. Let's look at light | Audience: Ages 4-8. | Audience: K to grade 3. | Includes bibliographical references and index.
Identifiers: LCCN 2018060251 | ISBN 9781977108951 (hardcover) | ISBN 9781977110428 (pbk.) | ISBN 9781977108999 (ebook pdf)
Subjects: LCSH: Light--Juvenile literature. | Sun--Juvenile literature.
Classification: LCC QC360 .S3835 2020 | DDC 535--dc23
LC record available at https://lccn.loc.gov/2018060251

Editorial Credits
Karen Aleo, editor; Kyle Grenz, designer; Tracy Cummins, media researcher; Laura Manthe, production specialist

Photo Credits
Shutterstock: Aphelleon, 11, Beautiful landscape, 9, Breadmaker, 5, Cathy Keifer, Cover Back, Edmund O'Connor, 6, Fer Gregory, 7, Harry Beugelink, 1, Iqbal Galuh Hartono, 19, Ivan Kovbasniuk, Cover Bottom, Klagyivik Viktor, 13, LeManna, 21, Pixel-Shot, 17, Sicio, Cover Top, sitthisak_k, 15

Note to Parents and Teachers

The Let's Look at Light set supports national standards related to light and energy. This book describes and illustrates sources of light. The images support early readers in understanding the text. The repetition of words and phrases helps early readers learn new words. This book also introduces early readers to subject-specific vocabulary words, which are defined in the Glossary section. Early readers may need assistance to read some words and to use the Table of Contents, Glossary, Read More, Internet Sites, Critical Thinking, and Index sections of the book.

All internet sites appearing in back matter were available and accurate when this book was sent to press.

Printed in China.
1654

Table of Contents

What Is Light?

Look at the bedroom. It's filled with light. Where is all the light coming from?

Light comes from many places. The sun, candles, and fireflies give off light. Light rays bounce off objects and travel to our eyes.

Light from Nature

Some light comes from nature. You see nature when you go outside. Nature is everything not made by people.

The sun gives us the most light. It's millions of miles away from Earth!

Yet it heats Earth too.

It's a huge ball of hot gas.

The moon is big and bright. But it doesn't make its own light. The moon reflects light from the sun.

See all the stars in the night sky. Stars are different sizes and colors. They shine as they give off light and heat.

Lights Made by People

Some lights are made
by people. People make
light bulbs. Light bulbs use
electricity to make light.
Lamps use light bulbs.

Candles give off small amounts of light and heat. A flame burns from the candle's wick. The wax near the flame melts.

Light Is All Around

Light is all around us. Indoors and in nature, light helps us see near and far. Light helps us see the world!

Glossary

electricity—a natural force that can be used to make light and heat or to make machines work

firefly—a small beetle that gives off light from its body; fireflies are also called lightning bugs

gas—something that is not solid or liquid and does not have a definite shape

nature—everything in the world that isn't made by people

ray—a line of light that beams out from something bright

reflect—to return light from an object; the moon reflects light from the sun

wick—a twisted cord in a candle

Read More

Bernhardt, Carolyn. *Light. Blastoff! Readers:* Science Starters. Minneapolis: Bellwether Media, 2019.

Braun, Eric. *Curious Pearl Investigates Light.* Curious Pearl, Science Girl. North Mankato, Minn.: Picture Window Books, a Capstone Imprint, 2018.

Spilsbury, Louise and Richard. *Sources of Light.* Exploring Light. Chicago: Heinemann Raintree, 2016.

Internet Sites

National Geographic Kids: Sun
https://kids.nationalgeographic.com/explore/space/sun/#sun.jpg

Ducksters: Physics for Kids: Science of Light
https://www.ducksters.com/science/light.php

Critical Thinking Questions

1. Name two items that use light bulbs.
2. How are we able to see the moon?
3. Describe how candles give off heat.

Index